FOREIGN
AFFAIRS

RENNAY CRAATS

Weigl Publishers Inc.

Published by Weigl Publishers Inc.
350 5th Avenue, Suite 3304, PMB 6G
New York, NY 10118-0069
Website: www.weigl.com

Library of Congress Cataloging-in-Publication Data

Craats, Rennay.
 Foreign affairs : USA past, present, future / Rennay Craats.
     p. cm.
 Includes index.
 ISBN 978-1-59036-978-4 (hard cover : alk. paper) -- ISBN 978-1-59036-979-1 (soft cover : alk. paper)
 1. United States--Foreign relations--Juvenile literature. I. Title.
 E183.7.C695 2009
 327.73--dc22

                              2008023865

Printed in the United States of America
1 2 3 4 5 6 7 8 9 0 12 11 10 09 08

All of the Internet URLs given in the book were valid at the time of publication. However, due to the
dynamic nature of the Internet, some addresses may have changed, or sites may have ceased to exist
since publication. While the author and publisher regret any inconvenience this may cause readers, no
responsibility for any such changes can be accepted by either the author or the publisher.

Weigl acknowledges Getty Images as its primary image supplier for this title.

Every reasonable effort has been made to trace ownership and to obtain permission to reprint copyright
material. The publishers would be pleased to have any errors or omissions brought to their attention so
that they may be corrected in subsequent printings.

EDITOR: Heather C. Hudak
DESIGN: Terry Paulhus

Foreign Affairs
Contents

Foreign Affairs
Through The Years

The United States is a powerful nation. It has vast natural resources, a large population, and access to advanced technology. However, to ensure the nation remains a respected leader, it must find ways to successfully work and communicate with neighboring countries.

Since the Declaration of Independence, the United States has had military, economic, and cultural relationships with many nations of the world. In the 20th century, the United States was a major influence in a number of global conflicts, from the world wars to the war on drugs.

The United States' involvement with the rest of the world has brought both great struggles and incredible successes. Through it all, the United States has continued to be dedicated to the ideals of democracy, freedom, and justice.

In the years to come, the United States will face many new challenges and opportunities. Climate change, dwindling resources, and political instability are just a few of the issues taking shape as we move deeper into the 21st century. Throughout history, the United States has proved that it can aptly adjust to and persevere in any new situation.

America Under Attack

On September 11, 2001, the United States found itself under attack. Four civilian airplanes, hijacked by members of the **terrorist** group al-Qaeda, were used as bombs. The first two planes struck the World Trade Center towers in New York City at 8:46 and 9:02 a.m., causing the buildings to collapse. A third plane crashed into the Pentagon at 9:36 a.m., though little wreckage of the plane could be found. The final aircraft was brought down by its passengers in a Pennsylvania field. They realized the hijackers likely had intended to crash the plane into the White House. The al-Qaeda group was led by Osama bin Laden, a member of a wealthy Saudi Arabian family that had been involved in business dealings with the United States for years. bin Laden had received money and training from the Central Intelligence Agency (CIA) when he helped fight off the Soviet invasion of Afghanistan in the 1980s. al-Qaeda believed that the United States had interfered with politics and people in the Middle East. In retaliation, al-Qaeda decided to attack the United States. These attacks had far-reaching effects on both the United States and the Middle East.

2001	2002	2003
The United States withdraws from the Anti-Ballistic Missile treaty.	President Bush begins referring to Iran, North Korea, and Iraq as an "axis of evil."	The United States invades Iraq.

2001

In the Aftermath

The attacks on September 11, 2001, inspired several actions by the U.S. government. Less than a month after the attacks, the United States, with the aid of Great Britain, invaded the nation of Afghanistan. This small country northwest of Pakistan was thought to be the location of Osama bin Laden and a large number of his al-Qaeda fighters. The rulers of Afghanistan at that time, the Taliban, were sympathetic to al-Qaeda and its goals, and had provided support and safe haven to the terrorists. The invasion succeeded in its goal of removing the Taliban from power, but failed to find and capture bin Laden. Fighting in Afghanistan continues, as United States, British, Canadian, French, German, and other allied forces keep the Taliban at bay and attempt to restore the well-being of the Afghan people. Another action taken by the U.S.

government after the attacks in September 2001 was to introduce a bill known as the USA PATRIOT Act, which stands for "Uniting and Strengthening America by Providing Appropriate Tools Required to Intercept and Obstruct Terrorism." The act gives law enforcement officials much greater freedom to pursue people believed to be terrorists. It also allows government agencies to listen to citizens' phone calls, read their emails, and look at medical and other records.

2003

The War in Iraq

On March 20, 2003, the United States invaded the nation of Iraq. Before the invasion, President George W. Bush stated that the leader of Iraq, Saddam Hussein, had access to powerful weapons and ties to the terrorists who had destroyed the Twin Towers in New York. However, when U.S. soldiers entered the country, they could not find the weapons or evidence of terrorist links. In 2007, the former chairman of the **Federal Reserve** Bank, Alan Greenspan, said that the Iraq war was largely about oil. Iraq controls a 112-billion-barrel supply of oil, making it one of the most oil-rich nations on Earth The United States consumes the most oil of any country, using about 8 billion barrels every year. More than 4,000 U.S. military personnel and over one million Iraqi civilians have been killed in the conflict.

The War in Iraq

2004

It is determined that there are no especially powerful weapons in Iraq.

2005

The United States rejects an international treaty designed to reduce the damage done to the environment by humans.

2004

Behind Bars Abroad

In order to prevent another terrorist attack on U.S. soil, many people around the world were imprisoned and interrogated by U.S. agencies, such as the military and CIA. These agencies hoped to learn information about terrorist plots and other activities that might be damaging to the United States. Many of these prisoners of the "war on terror" are held are at Guantanamo Bay in Cuba and Abu Ghraib in Iraq. In 2004, pictures were published showing prisoners in the Abu Ghraib facility being abused and tortured. Numerous soldiers and officers were removed from duty. President George W. Bush said that acts of human torture would not be tolerated. To date, several soldiers have been convicted of criminal offenses and discharged from the military.

2006

The Defense Cooperation Agreement between the United States and Bulgaria is signed.

2007

Bush announces plans for a U.S. military base in Africa.

2007

High-Tech Defense

In 2007, President George W. Bush campaigned for what he called a "missile shield" in eastern Europe. The shield would consist of several U.S. military bases in Poland and Czech Republic that could shoot down nuclear weapons launched by unfriendly nations. Russian President Vladimir Putin was opposed to this idea, saying that locating the bases so close to Russia was a threat to its security. The United States and Russia had been nuclear **adversaries** during the Cold War, and many worried that the construction of the missile shield would risk damaging the good relations that had developed in recent decades. Bush maintained that the missile

High-Tech Defense

bases were being set up to counter threats from Iran and that they would not to be used to bring harm to Russia.

However, Russia continued to oppose the plan, stating there would be negative consequences if the shield was installed.

Into the Future

As the United States entered the new millennium, it faced many challenges, including conflicts and large-scale acts of terrorism. Many people supported the actions of the government to combat these acts. Others were opposed. Think back throughout history to times when the people had different opinions about the direction of the nation, such as slavery and the Civil War. What can we learn from the past? How did people react?

2008

Presidential candidate Barack Obama suggests diplomacy abroad as an alternative to military action.

2009

2010

Foreign Affairs
1990s

U.S. Troops Defend Kuwait

captured more land. President Clinton proposed bombing Serb supply lines and getting rid of an embargo that prevented weapons from reaching the Muslims. No other European country would support his proposals. In 1994, the president continued to pressure European leaders to take action against the Serbs. In November, it seemed that the Serbs were about to take over Bosnian strongholds, so Clinton changed his mind. He decided to push for a settlement between the two sides. In 1995, Clinton hosted peace negotiations between Bosnia and Herzegovina. The Dayton peace accord resulted. This kept the country whole but as two separated areas. In addition, Clinton promised to send U.S. soldiers to Bosnia and Herzegovina to assist North Atlantic Treaty Organization (NATO) forces in providing aid and policing the area.

1991

U.S. Troops Defend Kuwait

President George H.W. Bush would not sit by and watch Iraq invade Kuwait in 1991. Within hours, he had contacted European, Asian, and Middle Eastern allies to help him stop Saddam Hussein. He even persuaded Saudi Arabia, which did not often allow foreign troops in its country, to allow U.S. soldiers to enter. Bush ordered the largest number of soldiers and supplies since the Vietnam War be sent to the Middle East. In January 1991, the U.S. Congress approved Bush's proposal for military action, and the U.S. and its allies invaded Kuwait. The air and ground battles lasted until February. When the war was over, Bush had reached his goal—he had limited U.S. casualties and had returned Kuwait to its own government's control.

1994

Clinton in Yugoslavia

After the breakup of Yugoslavia, the nation of Bosnia-Herzegovina was formed. A civil war in the area posed challenges for President Clinton. Bosnian Serb soldiers were better equipped than the Bosnian Muslims were, and they

Clinton in Yugoslavia

1991
The Soviet Union dissolves, and its member states become individual countries.

1992
U.S. troops land in Somalia in an attempt to stop violence between local groups.

1994

Aid to Africa

In his final weeks as president in 1994, George H.W. Bush sent U.S. soldiers to the East African country of Somalia. Somalis were starving to death while trying to survive a brutal civil war. The U.S. troops were to make sure that food and other supplies reached the people. Local armed groups in the dispute turned their fire on Americans, and many people at home questioned their soldiers' involvement. When Clinton took over as president, he realized the seriousness of the situation. Rather than pulling troops out, he doubled efforts to make sure that the U.S. forces could defend themselves and fulfill their mission. That did not sit well with citizens in the U.S. They demanded that the soldiers return home.

In March 1994, U.S. troops left Somalia, and UN troops took over their work. U.S. involvement in Africa in the 1990s was not over. A civil war in Rwanda in 1994 caused millions of people to flee. Disease and starvation claimed many lives in refugee camps in neighboring countries.

President Clinton sent food and supplies to the refugees in July. He also sent 200 soldiers to the capital city, Kigali, to make sure the relief supplies were delivered safely. The soldiers helped in the area until October. After all the relations with Africa, the Clintons decided to make a six-nation tour to the continent in 1998. It was the most extensive visit to Africa by a U.S. president and the first time a U.S. president had visited South Africa. Clinton hoped to promote trade and investment while highlighting the success stories in Africa.

1993

Many countries come together to begin work on the world's first international space station.

1994

The Rwanda Genocide happens.

1995

The U.S. get about 23 percent of imports from China and Japan.

1994

U.S. Actions in Haiti

American soldiers peacefully took over Haiti, an island in the Caribbean Sea, on September 19, 1994. The action started three years before when a military **coup** had taken over leadership from the country's first elected president, Jean-Bertrand Aristide. In 1993, President Clinton negotiated with the Haitian dictators in hopes of returning the former president. As part of the deal, the U.S. and the UN would help retrain the country's military and police forces. When the time came, the dictators went back on the deal. Anti-Aristide protestors blocked American and Canadian ships from reaching the docks, so they turned back. Clinton insisted that the regime step down and restore democracy and the elected president. The military government ignored the warnings. In 1994, a large American force entered Haiti. Clinton sent former president Jimmy Carter to speak to the military leader, Raoul Cédras, and persuade him to return control of the government and leave the country. Cédras finally agreed and handed back rule to Aristide. On October 13, Cédras and his lieutenants left Haiti, and two days later the Americans brought Aristide home. Democracy was restored but troops remained to smoothen the transition. American troops pulled out in 1995 and UN troops remained until December 1997. In 2004, U.S. forces removed Aristide from power, forcing him into exile in Africa.

1995

Being Neighborly

In 1995, the Mexican currency dropped quickly and many people feared that the country's economy would collapse. If that happened, the U.S. economy would suffer as well. President Clinton, together with Congress, tried to find a way to lessen the Mexican crisis. Congress refused to pass Clinton's plan to offer aid

1996
The G-7 Summit is held in France.

1997
The Kyoto Protocol is adopted by the 3rd Conference of the Parties.

1998
India and Pakistan test nuclear weapons.

Being Neighborly
Vice President Al Gore, U.S.
Treasury Secretary Robert
Rubin, President Bill Clinton,
and Mexican Ambassador
to the U.S. Silva Herzog

to Mexico. It did not think Americans would support this. Clinton did not give up. He created a $20 billion loan agreement with Mexico. The money would ease the anxiety of investors worldwide. This helped the Mexican economy recover.

In January 1997, Mexico finished paying back the loan to the U.S. It had done so three years ahead of schedule. A strong relationship with the U.S.'s southern neighbors was also apparent in 1996. Mexico and the U.S. joined forces in the war on drugs. Some members of Congress did not think that Mexico was doing

enough to stop the illegal drug trade. In 1997, a top Mexican official was arrested for protecting a drug trafficker. Despite this, Clinton maintained the partnership to put an end to the illegal drug trade. He visited Mexico in May 1997, but the controversy, along with conflict about U.S. immigration policies, created tension between the two countries.

Into the Future

In 1994, finding ways to aid Africans was a major focus of U.S. international relations. Providing aid to Africa is still an important issue. Research Africa online to find out more about the concerns that face Africans today. How can the United States help?

1999
NATO makes air strikes against Serbia in an attempt to defend an oppressed minority in that region.

2000
The first crew reaches the International Space Station.

Foreign Affairs
1980s

**Rocky Relationship
Muammar al-Qadhafi**

Rocky Relationship

In the 1980s, relations between Libya and the U.S. were strained. President Reagan thought that Libya's leader, Colonel Muammar al-Qadhafi, supported terrorists. The Libyan leader felt that the U.S. was trying to undermine his government. In 1981, Reagan increased U.S. military presence in countries neighboring Libya. U.S. troops shot down two Libyan planes that were attacking U.S. pilots. U.S. sources believe that al-Qadhafi tried to kill U.S. diplomats and planned to kill Reagan in retaliation. U.S. companies such as Exxon Oil withdrew from Libya. Reagan encouraged other U.S. businesses to leave, too. In March 1982, the government announced a boycott of Libyan oil. The loss of money caused problems for Libya. It pulled its forces out of Chad, where it had been supporting a civil war. This was the beginning of a rocky relationship between the U.S. and Libya.

1982

Conflict With Lebanon

On June 6, 1982, Israeli forces invaded and occupied Lebanon in an attempt to bring an end to the Palestine Liberation Organization (PLO), which had

1981

President Reagan offers aid to Saddam Hussein in his conflict with neighboring Iran.

1982

President Reagan sends U.S. marines to restore order in the nation of Libya.

been responsible for the deaths of many Israelis. During the occupation, pro-Israeli militias invaded Palestinian refugee camps and killed thousands of refugees. As well, many Lebanese civilians were killed by Israeli bombs in Lebanon's capital city, Beirut. International peacekeepers were unable to ease the conflict. It continued until 1985 when Israeli troops withdrew from some of the territory they had occupied. Israeli forces did not withdraw completely from Lebanon until 2000.

1983

Invasion of Grenada

The Caribbean island of Grenada became independent in 1974. Only five years later, the first prime minister was overthrown by Maurice Bishop. A second coup, and the murder of Bishop, occurred in 1983. There was great concern about the Marxist rebels that had taken power. On October 25, President Reagan and members of the Organization of East Caribbean States sent combat troops into the area. The troops remained there until the end of the year. An interim government was established in 1984, and fair elections were held. The invasion was viewed as a success in the U.S., but it was criticized by much of the rest of the world.

Conflict With Lebanon

Invasion of Grenada

1983
The U.S. removes Iraq from its list of nations that support terrorism.

1984
President Reagan asks other nations to ban chemical weapons.

1985
Mikhail Gorbachev becomes leader of the Soviet Union.

15

Free Trade
Canadian Prime Minister
Brian Mulroney and
President Ronald Reagan

1986

Free Trade

In 1986, Canadian Prime Minister Brian Mulroney and President Reagan began working on a trade agreement that would make it easier to buy and sell goods over the border. The leaders agreed to remove **tariffs** on goods crossing the border by 1988. They also agreed to take away investment restrictions that were in place. Canada and the U.S. were strong trade partners, and the deal would mean a boost to both countries' economies. Despite some initial debate, the agreement was signed. It paved the way for the North American Free Trade Agreement (NAFTA), which added Mexico to the agreement in 1994.

1989

The War on Drugs

In December 1989, President Bush sent troops into the Central American country of Panama. He wanted General Manuel Noriega arrested for drug trafficking. He also wanted to defend the 35,000 Americans who were living in Panama and defending the Panama Canal. Once Noriega was overthrown, Bush was friendly with the new leader, President Guillermo Endara. In 1990, Noriega turned himself in to U.S. officials and went to the U.S. to stand trial. He was convicted of drug trafficking in 1992 and sentenced to 40 years in prison.

▲The War on Drugs
Panamanian President
Guillermo Endara and President
George Bush

1986

The United Nations declares 1986 the International Year of Peace.

1987

U.S. warships in the Persian Gulf destroy two Iranian patrol boats.

Comrades With Russia President George Bush and USSR President Mikhail Gorbachev

1989

Comrades With Russia

President George H.W. Bush kept up the good relations with the USSR that Ronald Reagan had begun. In 1989, Bush and USSR President Mikhail Gorbachev met on a Soviet ship near the coast of Malta. The two leaders discussed the rapid changes that were happening in Europe. While they did not come to any formal agreements, both sides acknowledged the importance of cooperation. The following year, the leaders met in the U.S. Both agreed to destroy their chemical weapons in the name of world peace. Throughout his term as president, George Bush continued to encourage economic relationships with the USSR.

Into the Future

Since Ronald Reagan and Mikhail Gorbachev first began peaceful relations in the 1980s, Russia and the United States have worked together in a number of ways. Research how these two nations overcame the Cold War and the projects they have tackled since. How can Russia and the United States ensure their good relations continue into the future?

President George W. Bush and Vladimir Putin

1988
The House of Representatives rejects Reagan's request for funds to support Nicaraguan Contras.

1989
The Cold War ends with the fall of the Berlin Wall.

1990
Iraq invades its neighbor Kuwait.

Foreign Affairs
1970s

CIA Assassins
Cuban Premier Fidel Castro and
Chilean President Salvador Allende

East Meets West

After twenty years of disagreeing with each other, the People's Republic of China and the U.S. came together. President Nixon began to repair a strained relationship between China and the U.S. on June 10, 1971, when he announced that he would drop the decades-old trade embargo against China. Then on February 21, 1972, Nixon became the first U.S. president to meet with Chinese **communists**. President Nixon and Secretary of State Henry Kissinger met with Chinese Premier Zhou Enlai and Chairman Mao Zedong to discuss issues, including the threat of the Soviet Union. The trip did not accomplish much in the way of trade agreements, but the leaders promised to join together to work toward world peace.

1970s

CIA Assassins

In the 1970s, it was alleged that the Central Intelligence Agency (CIA) was linked to assassinations and the coup in Chile. The U.S. reportedly spent $13.5 million to get the Chilean president, Salvador Allende, out of office. The agency financed an anti-Allende newspaper and was said to have encouraged the 1973 coup in which Allende was killed. There were additional reports that the CIA had plotted to kill Premier Patrice Lumumba of Zaire and Fidel Castro of Cuba. It was also suggested that the agency encouraged or knew about coups that killed Vietnamese President Ngo Dinh Diem, Chilean General Rene Schneider, and dictator Rafael Trujillo of the Dominican Republic. Frank Church's Senate panel revealed these events in a report. As a result of these accusations, the government established permanent committees to watch over CIA operations.

East Meets West
President Richard Nixon and Chinese
Prime Minister, Zhou Enlai

1971

The Seabed Treaty makes it illegal to use nuclear weapons on the ocean floor.

1972

The United States gives Okinawa back to Japan.

1972

Withdrawal from Vietnam

On March 30, 1972, more than 30,000 North Vietnamese troops crossed the **neutral** zone and attacked Quang Ti Province in South Vietnam. In response to this attack, President Nixon ordered a bombing campaign against North Vietnamese troops. Nixon continued the offensive for seven months, after which at least 100,000 communist troops lay dead. Talks were set up to bring an end to the fighting. An end to America's longest war was in sight. U.S. Secretary of State, Henry Kissinger, and Le Duc Tho, the North Vietnam representative, agreed to a cease-fire and withdrawal, but South Vietnam's Nguyen van Thieu was not happy. He accused the U.S. of selling out his country. Nixon refused to sign the agreement. After more bombings, both sides returned to the negotiations. On January 27, 1973, the Vietnam War ended with the signing of the Treaty of Paris. By March 29, all U.S. troops were out of Vietnam. On paper, the war was over, but fighting continued in Vietnam until 1975, when the North defeated the South.

1973
A peace agreement is reached with Vietnam.

1974
Spokane, Washington, hosts the Expo '74 World's Fair.

1975
Cambodian forces take control of the U.S. ship *Mayaguez*.

1972

Warming the Cold War

Richard Nixon became the first U.S. president to visit the USSR. In 1972, Nixon met with the Soviet leader, Leonid Brezhnev, in Moscow. The meeting was a great success. The two leaders discussed trade, arms control, and scientific cooperation. The most noteworthy agreements to come of the visit were the treaties known as SALT I and SALT II, in which Nixon and Brezhnev agreed to limit the number of their missiles and nuclear weapons. They also discussed having joint projects in space. This came about in 1975, with the Apollo-Soyuz space docking. While some Americans were skeptical of the new friendship, many were thankful that the Cold War was thawing.

1979

Hostages in Iran

In 1979, 500 Iranian students backed by Ayatollah Khomeini, Iran's religious leader, invaded the U.S. Embassy in Tehran, Iran. They took ninety hostages. The revolutionaries were angry that the U.S. had allowed the **Shah** of Iran to have surgery in American hospitals. President Carter froze all Iranian assets in U.S. banks and sent a task force to the Indian Ocean so that it would be within attacking distance of Iran. Horrified Americans watched as blindfolded marines appeared on television with their hands bound. Around them, Iranians chanted "Death to America! Death to the Shah!" The terrorists demanded that the Shah be sent back to them. Carter tried to negotiate but had little success. A few hostages, mostly women and African Americans, were released, leaving fifty-two captives. An evacuation was attempted, but it failed, and eight people were killed. The remaining hostages were released on January 20, 1981.

Warming the Cold War
Soviet leader Leonid Brezhnev
and President Richard Nixon

1976

The United States rejects the UN's call to make an independent Palestinian state.

1977

Jimmy Carter pardons Vietnam War draft dodgers.

1978

Volkswagon is the first non-U.S. carmaker to open a U.S. plant.

Hostages in Iran

Into the Future

In the 1970s, President Richard Nixon took the first steps toward bridging the gap between the United States and countries like Russia and China. How do you think these actions shaped the relationship the United States has with these countries today?

President Richard Nixon

1979
The United States funds the Islamic resistance, led by Osama bin Laden, to the Soviet invasion of Afghanistan.

1980
President Carter and the European Commission enact a grain embargo against the USSR.

Foreign Affairs
1960s

Spy Disaster
Gary Powers

Spy Disaster

The relationship between the Soviet Union and the U.S. was at an all-time low in the sixties. Throughout the fifties, U.S. spy planes had flown over the Soviet Union, but the USSR could not do anything about it. Their early missiles did not have the power to reach the planes. By the sixties, technology had advanced, and the Soviets had caught up to the U-2 planes. On May 1, 1960, Central Intelligence Agency pilot Gary Powers was shot down while flying over the Soviet Union in a spy plane. President Eisenhower and his government tried to explain away the incident, which came at a terrible time. It was a few weeks before a Four Powers summit meeting was to take place in Paris. The Cold War became a few degrees colder. Premier Khrushchev made an announcement on May 5, but he did not say that the pilot had been taken from the wreckage alive. U.S. officials tried to claim that the aircraft was a civilian one that had accidentally entered Soviet airspace. Then the premier played his ace-in-the-hole. Powers had confessed to spying. Eisenhower tried to patch things up enough to move ahead with the Paris summit, but not even the promise of no more U-2 spy planes could appease Khrushchev. He suggested

1961
The Berlin Wall is built by the USSR.

1962
The United States provides military aid to South Vietnam.

1963
The United States, the Soviet Union and Great Britain, sign a nuclear test ban treaty.

that Eisenhower be **impeached**. The summit was called off. Powers was tried for spying and sentenced to ten years in a Soviet prison. Many Americans did not feel sorry for him—they did not respect that he had confessed and pleaded guilty to the charges. Regardless, in 1962, the U.S. government traded Powers for the Soviet spy Rudolph Abel, who had been arrested in the U.S.

1960

U.S.-Japan Treaty

The close relationship between Japan and the U.S. after World War II caused tension between Japan and communist countries. In 1960, the U.S. and Japan met to renegotiate the 1952 mutual-security treaty. This had been signed after Japan had reclaimed its **sovereignty**. The revised agreement stated that the U.S. could keep its military bases in Japan and could become involved against foreign or communist aggression in the area. Many Japanese people were against the treaty because it made a trade relationship with Japan's communist neighbors nearly impossible. Demonstrations flared as students protested Japanese support of U.S. foreign policy.

1963

Cooler Heads Prevail

Relations between the Soviet Union and Communist China had begun to sour, and the U.S. took advantage of the situation and reopened communications with the USSR. The Soviets decided to help ease international tensions about nuclear war, especially after the Cuban Missile Crisis. On August 5, 1963, the U.S., Great Britain, and the Soviet Union agreed on a treaty that would ban atomic weapons testing in the atmosphere, in space, and underwater. Testing underground, however, was not banned. President Kennedy and Premier Khrushchev installed a "hotline" for easy communication between the two countries. In case of an emergency, the two heads of state could contact each other directly. This agreement helped calm fears of nuclear disaster in the U.S. and around the world. It also brought the feuding countries a step closer together.

U.S.-Japan Treaty
Prime Minister of Japan Kishi Nobusuke, Christian A. Herter, and Douglas MacArthur II

Cooler Heads Prevail
President John F. Kennedy and Nikita Khrushchev

1964

The Gulf of Tonkin incident spurs U.S. military action in Vietnam.

1965

Fidel Castro allows one million Cuban citizens to immigrate to the United States.

1965

Dominican Republic

On April 24, 1965, an army group rebelled against the government of the Dominican Republic. Four days later, U.S. marines landed in the area. Many American citizens lived there, so President Johnson sent 22,000 U.S. troops to the country to protect them. The troops were also there to prevent a Communist government from taking control of the country. U.S. forces stationed themselves between the rebel-occupied parts of Santo Domingo and the areas run by government loyalists. In May, a cease-fire was established, and U.S. troops took on peacekeeping duties. The following month, the marines left the Dominican Republic, but 12,500 other soldiers stayed. The U.S. presence in the Dominican Republic caused anti-American feelings in many parts of the world, and many people within the U.S. criticized the decision to enter the country as well.

1966
Vietnam protests are held across the United States.

1967
CIA assassins locate and kill Che Guevara, a leader of the Cuban revolution.

1968
The North Vietnamese and guerillas join forces to attack U.S. troops.

Dominican Republic

1968

Failed Peace in Vietnam

President Johnson tried to move ahead with peace negotiations to end the Vietnam War in 1968. He had little success. The peace talks in Paris broke down in May after disagreements about the status of the National Liberation Front (NLF), a communist group in South Vietnam. The South Vietnamese government in Saigon refused to recognize the NLF. In October, just before the U.S. presidential election, candidate Hubert Humphrey pushed for a peace settlement. Richard Nixon secretly convinced South Vietnamese President Nguyen Van Thieu to wait for better terms that would materialize once Nixon was elected. Thieu announced that he would not negotiate with communists, bringing the peace talks to a screeching halt. Nixon did not have any more luck

Failed Peace in Vietnam
President Richard Nixon

when he took over the peace talks. Neither side would alter its position. The communists insisted that all U.S. troops leave Vietnam. They also demanded that the Saigon government be removed and replaced via an election that included the NLF government party. Peace talks fell apart and both sides continued fighting the war.

Into the Future

Finding a resolution to a conflict that all parties involved agree upon can be a huge challenge. President Johnson learned this first hand in 1968. Think about a time you have had a conflict with someone. How do you overcome this obstacle?

President Lyndon B. Johnson

1969
SALT I negotiations between the United States and the Soviet Union take place in Helsinki, Finland.

1970
The United States begins an invasion of Cambodia.

1951

Supporting Coups

In 1951, Iran decided to nationalize the British-owned Anglo-Iranian Oil Company. London asked the U.S. to help. Negotiations failed, and the British looked to the U.S. to support a boycott of Iranian oil. President Truman was not sure if he should support the Iranians or his ally's interests. His **successor**, Dwight Eisenhower,

did not face the same problem. He feared Iran would become communist, so he stepped in. The boycott crippled Iran's economy and its nationalist party. To maintain control, Muhammad Mussadegh, Iran's premier, was given special government powers. He now counted on the support of the communist Tudeh Party, which was becoming more and more powerful. In 1953, when Mussadegh insisted that the Shah be ousted, even the Tudeh

turned against him. The time was perfect for President Eisenhower and British Prime Minister Churchill to act. The Shah had ordered Mussadegh to resign, but he refused to go. His followers rebelled, and the Shah fled. The Central Intelligence Agency (CIA) took charge of the coup and orchestrated a military revolt. In the course of a week of street fighting, 300 Iranians died, Mussadegh was arrested, and the Shah returned. Immediately, Iran was ruled by the military. The Anglo-Iranian Oil Company became an international group, and the U.S. held a major stake in the organization. Throughout Iran, anti-American feelings spread and grew stronger.

Supporting Coups

1951
Nuclear testing begins at the Nevada Test Site.

1952
The United States signs a peace treaty with Japan.

1953
The Korean war is ended with the signing of an armistice agreement.

Meetings in Geneva
President Dwight D. Eisenhower
and James C. Haggerty

1955

Meetings in Geneva

In 1955, the world was settling into post-war life. In May, the USSR agreed to the Austrian State Treaty. This gave Austria its independence, and Soviet troops withdrew from the area.

This occupation had been a sore point between the East and West. In July, leaders from Great Britain, France, and the U.S. met with the Soviet leader in Geneva, Switzerland, to talk about how Austria and the USSR could live together peacefully. President Eisenhower announced

that he did not intend to participate in an aggressive war. This relieved citizens of the world. Many feared a nuclear war. The conference also discussed the feeling of hopefulness in the USSR after Stalin's death. In the end, no substantial agreements were reached at these meetings.

1954

The Berlin Conference takes place.

1955

President Eisenhower sends advisors to South Vietnam.

1956

Khrushchev Begins Thaw

Soviet leader Nikita Khrushchev made a speech in February 1956 about the crimes of Stalin, the dictator who had died in 1953. Until then, no public criticism of the leader had been permitted. Khrushchev spoke of Stalin as a mass murderer and a power-hungry leader who ruled by terror and betrayed communism and the USSR. Khrushchev's "secret speech" addressed Stalin's deportation of many national minorities back to their homelands.

Khrushchev condemned Stalin for his illegal deeds and the effects his actions had on Soviets. Khrushchev's speech marked the beginning of his de-Stalinization efforts. He wanted to improve the standard of living and give citizens more freedom. The secret police became less important to government operations. The USSR, however, remained a communist country. Many people in the West hoped that Khrushchev's new vision would help open relations between the U.S. and the USSR.

1959

The Kitchen Debate

In 1959, Vice President Richard Nixon and Soviet Premier Nikita Khrushchev exchanged heated words in what was to be called the "Kitchen Debate." Nixon flew to Moscow in July to open the American National Exhibition. This was an unusual Soviet presentation of U.S. culture. The visit came just after the U.S. Congress had passed the Captive Nations Resolution, which criticized the Soviet government for the way it treated the countries under its control. Before heading to the exhibition, the two politicians met. The discussion quickly turned into an argument about the U.S. resolution. The men then left to tour the exhibition grounds separately. They met again in the kitchen of a model U.S.

home. Khrushchev made fun of the gadgets, including juicers and dishwashers, and said he figured U.S. workers could not afford these luxuries. Nixon struck back, saying that the average American could easily live in this model home. The conversation turned into a debate about communism versus capitalism, right there in the kitchen. Before then, world statesmen had rarely spoken to one another so sharply or so honestly.

Khrushchev Begins Thaw

1956
North and South Vietnam begin a civil war.

1957
Nuclear testing in the United States is put on hold for two years.

1958
The North American Aerospace Defense Command is signed.

The Kitchen Debate
Nikita Khrushchev and Vice
President Richard Nixon

Into the Future

The United States has always been a democracy. However, there are many different types of governments. Research the types of governments found in other countries around the world. What are some of the strong features of these types of governments? What are their weak points? How are they different from a democracy?

1959
The St. Lawrence Seaway opens.

1960
The United States and Japan sign the Treaty of Mutual Cooperation and Security.

29

1941

Great Ambitions

In December 1941, President Roosevelt, British Prime Minister Winston Churchill, and their respective advisors gathered in Washington to discuss how they were going to end the war. They agreed that Hitler had to be stopped first, and the battle with Japan would be a U.S. matter. The leaders decided to create a top-level military committee made up of both British and American members. This committee would work in Washington to plan military strategies. Then on January 1, 1942, officials from the U.S., Britain, the Soviet Union, and 23 other countries met and agreed to work together to end the war. They would not negotiate separately with the Axis powers. The peace that the Allies promised would be delivered to everyone. Churchill, Roosevelt, and Stalin met in February 1945. They planned the final attacks on the Axis powers and discussed Europe's future. In return for Stalin's support in defeating Japan, he was promised several territories, including the return of the Kurile Islands and part of Manchuria, which the Soviet Union had lost to Japan in 1875 and 1904. As well, Churchill and Roosevelt called for democracy in Eastern Europe, a declaration that Stalin ignored.

1944

Iron Curtain Descends

In 1944, the Soviet Union went from being a victim of Germany to a victor over Germany. Prime Minister Churchill was worried about what would happen once the war was over. He feared that many of the countries would become communist if the Soviet Union had its way. Churchill tried to bring the U.S. on board with his attempt to block Soviet influence. President Roosevelt was not interested in getting involved. Churchill met with Stalin about how to split up the Balkans region. Churchill wanted to let Stalin control Romania and Bulgaria, while Great Britain took control of Greece. The two would split Yugoslavia and Hungary fifty-fifty. The deal was never finalized. President Roosevelt, on the other hand, accepted Soviet expansion. He felt that both countries had interests, and they could work them out later. Churchill was disappointed with the lack of alarm in the U.S. Without Roosevelt's military support, Churchill had no other choice than to watch the Soviet army take control of Poland, Romania, Bulgaria, Hungary, and Czechoslovakia.

Great Ambitions
Winston Churchill, Franklin Roosevelt, and Joseph Stalin

1941
The attack on Pearl Harbor draws the United States into World War II.

1942
Thailand declares war on Great Britain and the United States.

1943
Roosevelt and Winston Churchill discuss European war strategy.

1944
The Marshall Islands are
invaded by U.S. forces.

1945
At the end of World War II, Germany is
divided into Western and Soviet sections.

authority, but it soon became obvious that such a system would not work. After six weeks of discussions, the United Nations was created. This organization was to have a general assembly of countries dedicated to peace. There would be a powerful executive council run by the permanent members, which were initially the four powers. Over the next year, details were worked out, and 50 nations came together to promote economic development, world peace, and the protection of human rights. In 1948, the countries of North and South America met in Colombia to establish the Organization of American States (OAS). This organization promised mutual security for American countries. The OAS was the first regional defense bloc under the United Nations.

1948

NATO Established

Britain, Luxembourg, France, the Netherlands, and Belgium signed a collective defense agreement in 1948. This alliance needed the military and financial support of the U.S. The North Atlantic Treaty Organization (NATO) talks began immediately, and in 1949, 12 Western countries, including the U.S. and Canada, signed the North Atlantic Treaty. The treaty stated that an attack on one member country would be an attack on all of them. Leaders hoped that, allied in this

The World Unites

1944

The World Unites

Representatives from the four big powers—the U.S., Great Britain, the USSR, and China—gathered in Washington, D.C., in 1944. They wanted to find a way to prevent another world war. They worked toward an international organization that would help solve conflicts without war. The four powers wanted to hold most

1946
The French conflict in Vietnam begins.

1947
The Truman Doctrine is declared to halt the spread of communism from Russia.

1948
President Truman enacts the second peacetime military draft.

NATO Established
President Harry S. Truman

way, their countries would be able to defend themselves against the growing influence of the Soviet Union. The Soviets were taking over Eastern and Central Europe. U.S. officials called NATO the "antidote to fear," but the establishment of NATO completed the separation of the world into two armed camps.

Into the Future

The development of NATO ensured that certain nations would remain allies in the face of wartime threat and also ensure that no one nation take a stand against another. Since NATO was signed, have any other countries banded together in a similar way? What countries might benefit from putting such a treaty into effect? Why?

1949
The USSR detonates its first atomic weapon, beginning an arms race with the United States.

1950
United Nations forces, led by U.S. troops, prevent a Chinese takeover of Korea.

Foreign Affairs
1930s

1930

Hoover's Push for Peace

President Hoover thought the U.S. should not get involved in other countries' wars. At the 1930 London Naval Conference, the U.S. made an agreement with Great Britain and Japan to limit the size and number of warships they built. Hoover also took part in the world disarmament conference in Geneva, Switzerland, in 1932. Later, he laid the foundation for what Roosevelt would call the Good Neighbor Policy. Hoover insisted that the U.S. consider the Latin American countries' interests as well as its own. As the Depression took hold of Latin American countries, governments were overthrown, and Hoover accepted the new governments, whatever they were. Again, President Hoover's disapproval of conflict shone through when Japan invaded Manchuria. The secretary of state wanted the president to impose harsh sanctions against Japan, but the president would not go any further than expressing disapproval for Japan's invasion.

Hoover's Push for Peace

1931

Under the Stimson Doctrine, the U.S. refuses to recognize the Japanese takeover of certain Chinese territories.

1932

Ninety percent of the debt owed by Germany for its actions in World War I is cancelled.

Standing Alone
President Franklin Roosevelt

1933

Standing Alone

President Roosevelt's policies seemed to some those of an **isolationist**. Before him, Herbert Hoover had guaranteed that the U.S. would be at the International Economic Conference in London, England, in the summer of 1933, so Roosevelt kept the promise. Although he attended, he did not think everyone there would be able to agree on how to end the Depression. Many of his advisers lacked faith in the European bankers and convinced him that it would not be a good idea for the U.S. economy to be tied to an international agreement. So Roosevelt decided that the U.S. would look after itself. Many citizens agreed. They blamed the Depression on the after-effects of World War I, and they supported their president's isolationism. Many laws aimed at keeping the U.S. neutral were passed during this time. However, as the thirties passed, President Roosevelt could not ignore what was happening in the rest of the world.

1933
The "Good Neighbor Policy" is developed to prevent armed actions by foreign powers in the Americas.

1934
U.S. troops leave Haiti.

1935
The Neutrality Act prohibits all shipments of arms abroad.

Roosevelt Takes Action

U.S. on the Sidelines
Adolf Hitler

1936

Roosevelt Takes Action

President Roosevelt was concerned about the faltering world peace in the mid-thirties. In 1936, the president sailed to Buenos Aires, Argentina, to take part in an International American Conference for Peace. He told the people there that if a non-American country attacked any American country, they should all pull together in resisting the **aggressor**. Less than a year after this meeting, Roosevelt spoke out against Japan's attacks on China. He suggested that any country that attacked another should be **quarantined**. While nothing came of this suggestion, it showed the way the president was thinking. As Germany and Japan became bolder and more aggressive, the president asked for more than $1 billion to expand the navy. Despite

Roosevelt's vow not to become involved in conflicts, he built up U.S. defenses as a precaution.

1939

U.S. on the Sidelines

Americans read newspaper accounts of Hitler's attack on Poland in 1939. Britain and France declared war on Germany. The U.S. did not. It stayed neutral. President Roosevelt promised that he would do everything he could to keep U.S. troops out of the war in Europe. He did, however, support those countries fighting against the aggressors. Though at first he was not allowed to sell them arms, the 1939 "cash and carry" law changed the situation. It allowed the U.S. to sell arms if the buyers paid cash and used their own ships to transport the weapons. As a result, Great Britain and France could buy war supplies in the U.S. Then the government gave Britain 50

destroyers in return for being allowed to have air and naval bases on British land. As the war got worse and Hitler took more territory, the president began to strengthen U.S. defenses. The country stayed out of the fighting until 1941, when the Japanese bombed Pearl Harbor.

1936
Nazi Germany regains control over the Rhineland.

1937
Franklin Roosevelt is sworn in for a second term as president.

1938
Churchill asks western Europe and the Americas to prepare for war.

Into the Future

Throughout history, the United States has played a key role in conflicts around the world. However, at the outset of World War II, the nation decided to remain neutral. Are there any current conflicts taking place in the world that the United States has decided not to take part in? Why?

1939

The United States declares that it will remain neutral in the war.

1940

Axis Powers align against France and Great Britain.

Foreign Affairs
1920s

1920s

Control of Nicaragua

The U.S. had been involved in Nicaragua since the turn of the century. For the first part of the 1900s, the U.S. supported a conservative government in Nicaragua. U.S. marines were stationed there to protect the government from a coup. As long as a conservative government was in place, U.S. businesses were protected. In the early 1920s, the U.S. government wanted to make Nicaragua more secure so that the marines could pull out. It trained a professional military to guarantee fair elections and keep order in the country. The elections brought a weak government into power in 1925. The marines left and civil war broke out. When the defeated Conservative candidate, General Emiliano Chamorro, took over the government, the U.S. forced him from office. Adolfo Díaz, the former Conservative president, then took over. In 1927, after much civil unrest, thousands of marines landed in Nicaragua to support Díaz's government. The marines stayed in Nicaragua until 1933. When they left, they passed the responsibilities to the U.S.-trained National Guard. American involvement in Nicaragua strained U.S.—Latin American relations for decades.

Control of Nicaragua

1921
The United States officially ends World War I.

1922
The Five Power Naval Disarmament Treaty is signed.

1923
One U.S. dollar has a value of 4.2 quadrillion German papiermark.

League of Nations

League of Nations

On November 15, 1920, the League of Nations met for the first time. The man behind the agency, President Woodrow Wilson, was not there. He had dreamed of such an international organization that would work for peace and disarmament. Members of the League promised to respect each other's territory. If a conflict arose, the other members would help the involved parties discuss the issue and bring it to a non-violent conclusion. The U.S. government failed to pass the Treaty of Versailles, which held the League's bill. Wilson himself had encouraged senators to vote "no" because of changes to the bill made by the Republican Senator Henry Cabot Lodge. While campaigning against the bill, Wilson suffered a stroke. Republican Warren Harding was nominated to run in the 1920 election, and he won. In his inaugural address, Harding told Americans that he would not become involved in conflicts in Europe.

1924

The United States leads a conference to ease Germany's responsibilities after World War I and improve its economy.

1925

Benito Mussolini becomes dictator in Italy.

1921

Paying for Panama

In 1903, the U.S. helped Panama rebel against Colombia to become a separate country. The 1903 rebellion was spurred by the Colombian government's refusal to allow the U.S. to complete and run the Panama Canal. Panama received payment from the U.S. for this right, and it was time to pay Colombia too. In April 1921, the U.S. Senate approved a treaty with Colombia. In the treaty, the U.S. government agreed to pay Colombia $25 million to recognize Panama's independence. Senator Henry Cabot Lodge encouraged the U.S. government to pay the sum to settle the bitterness between Colombia and the U.S. He also hoped that it would help the government negotiate drilling rights for American companies with operations in Colombia.

1921

The Cost of War

In January 1921, the Allies—including Great Britain, France, and the U.S.—presented Germany with the bill for World War I.

Germany was blamed for the war and was ordered to pay damages. The U.S. claimed the "rights and advantages" won by the Allies in the Treaty of Versailles. The U.S. would not, however, accept any responsibilities assumed by the Allies. The next step was to collect the payments from Germany. The Allies made demands, but Germany suggested lower amounts. So Allied troops entered Germany to prove they were serious about their demands. In March, Germany reluctantly offered $32 billion to compensate the Allies for the war. This fine was higher than any country had paid

1926
The League of Nations allows Germany to join.

1927
The population of the world is two billion.

1928
The United States pulls its troops out of China.

The Cost of War

ever before. The settlement depended on the agreement of the German people. The National Socialist German Workers' Party—the Nazi Party—rebelled against it.

They interrupted political meetings and threatened those in favor of paying the fine. In the end, Germany reduced the size of its military to 100,000 soldiers,

and recognized the sovereignty of Poland, Belgium, and Czechoslovakia. It did not, however, pay the fine.

Into the Future

The League of Nations was eventually replaced by the United Nations. Over time, this organization has grown and changed to include many new departments and goals. What are the objectives of the United Nations? How is the UN today different from the League of Nations? How are they the same?

1929

A plan to preserve Niagara Falls is put in place by the United States and Canada.

1930

The Smoot-Hawley Tariff Act is signed into law.

1910s

Mixed Messages

President Wilson concentrated on America's relationship with other countries. He began an agreement that offered Colombia a $20 million payment for the role America had played in Panama's revolt against Colombia. The agreement became final in 1921. This brought anger from former President Theodore Roosevelt, who had encouraged Panama to break away from Colombia and become independent. Roosevelt resented Wilson's virtual apology for his previous policy. Regardless, President Wilson's government wanted to show that it wished to

Mixed Messages
William Jennings Bryan

maintain friendly relations within North and South America. Some of Wilson's actions did not support this claim of goodwill. Wilson and his secretary of state, William Jennings Bryan, approved actions that threatened Nicaragua's independence. They wanted to build a new canal, and they feared that the part of Nicaragua best suited for a canal would be taken over by European powers. In 1913, the U.S. government drafted a treaty that restricted the actions of the Nicaraguan government and allowed for U.S. involvement in the area. This **imperialistic** move was criticized by many people because it carried on President Taft's policies in the area. A year earlier, Marines had arrived in Nicaragua to stop a revolt against the U.S.-backed president, Adolfo Diaz. They remained there until 1933.

1914

Close to War

In 1914, Mexican leader Venustiano Carranza overthrew President Huerta, but that did not help U.S. interests in the country. The new leader would not abide by the findings of mediators who were investigating the Veracruz

Close to War
Victoriano Huerta

killings. Wilson then turned his eyes to opposition leader Francisco "Pancho" Villa. That did not work out either. Villa tried to get the U.S. to invade Mexico so that he could take power. To anger the U.S. government into action, he raided U.S. towns near the border. In October 1915, Wilson decided to recognize Carranza as leader of Mexico. Villa reacted by kidnapping and killing Americans in January 1916. Then, he crossed the border into Columbus, New Mexico. There, he murdered U.S. citizens and set the town on fire. Wilson responded by sending 6,000 troops to Mexico and had Carranza's permission to search for Villa. Villa escaped and crossed the border again. He killed more Americans in Glen Springs, Texas. This almost caused a war between the countries. To calm the situation, a constitutional government was established in October 1916. Wilson brought his troops home, but relations between the neighbors were strained.

1911
Canada pulls out of the Reciprocity Treaty with the U.S.

1916
The U.S. establishes a new military government in the Dominican Republic.

Trouble South of the Border

1914

Trouble South of the Border

Since 1910, Mexico had experienced revolution after revolution. Americans with property or businesses there wanted the government to send troops in to protect their interests. Instead, President Wilson decided to protect U.S. interests by encouraging a constitutional government in Mexico. Wilson would not recognize Mexico's leader, General Victoriano Huerta, because he had taken power illegally. The U.S. supported Venustiano Carranza, who gained political strength with this U.S. backing. Regardless, Huerta maintained control. In April 1914, U.S. sailors were arrested at Tampico by Huerta's security force. The men were released, but Wilson was enraged. He demanded apologies from Huerta's government, even though he would not recognize it. When the U.S. discovered that a German ship full of ammunition was on its way to the Mexican leader, Wilson sent troops to Veracruz. In the clash that followed, more than 300 Mexicans and 90 Americans were killed or wounded. Immediately, public opinion in Mexico turned against the U.S.

1919

Treaty of Versailles

At the end of World War I, Germany and the Allies signed an agreement called the Treaty of Versailles. The details of the peace agreement were negotiated at the Paris Peace Conference beginning January 18, 1919. The U.S., Great Britain, France, and Italy all attended the conference. Even though the decision would affect Germany greatly, there was no representative from that country at the meetings. In the first part of the treaty was the Covenant of the League of Nations. This created the first global peacekeeping organization. The league would enforce the decisions and negotiations that arose from treaties after World War I. The Treaty of Versailles ordered Germany to give up 10 percent of its territory to France and Poland and to pay damages to France and Belgium. Among other conditions, Germany had to agree to reduce the size of its military. Germans were generally unhappy with the agreement. It remained a source of anger for 20 years, and this anger led to World War II. The treaty was ratified on June 28, 1919. The U.S., however, did not sign the agreement. Instead, it signed a separate Treaty of Peace with Germany on August 25, 1921, in Berlin.

Treaty of Versailles

1916

The United States and Nicaragua sign a treaty outlining the future construction of a canal.

1917

The United States enters World War I.

1919

The United States does not join the League of Nations. 43

Foreign Affairs
1900s

Cuba in Dispute

1900

Cuba in Dispute

American troops had occupied Cuba since the end of the Spanish-American War in 1898. The countries agreed that the U.S. would control Cuba, and by 1899, American troops had taken over. The U.S. kept its promise to allow Cuba to govern itself, but only by those leaders who followed democratic rules and were "Americanized." Despite American efforts to control the government, Cuban separatists won a majority of the seats in the assembly in 1900. To make sure that American interests were protected, the U.S. Government insisted that the new constitution define the relationship between the U.S. and Cuba. These conditions led to the passing of the Platt Amendment. Under this, Cuba could not make treaties or alliances with other countries, it had to allow U.S. military bases on the island, and it had to agree that the U.S. could intervene on the island in times of crisis. The U.S. Government refused to pull troops from Cuba until these conditions were met, so the Platt Amendment was placed in the Cuban constitution. After a great deal of opposition and debate, the amendment was passed by a margin of one vote. Many Cubans resented the amendment. They saw it as an assault on their independence. Anti-American feelings swept Cuba. U.S. troops left Cuba in 1902.

1901

Taking Panama

In 1901, Great Britain and the U.S. negotiated the Hay-Pauncefote Treaty. This agreement was arranged in order to build and manage a canal across the **isthmus** of Panama. The U.S. Senate would not pass the treaty unless it said that the U.S. could do whatever it needed to defend the canal zone. It also wanted to delete a clause about the involvement of other nations in the area's neutrality. Britain objected to these changes, and another draft was created and submitted to the Senate. This one passed. It stated that the U.S. had control of building and managing the canal. The U.S. also was to be responsible for guaranteeing neutrality, which included building fortifications. The canal was to be available to all nations equally, but the U.S. could restrict its use in times of war. In 1911, Great Britain said that the U.S. had maneuvered around the last point by passing the Panama Canal Act. This **exempted** Americans from paying canal tolls. President Wilson agreed and repealed the act in 1914.

Taking Panama

1900
U.S. troops take part in the Boxer Rebellion.

1901
The Hay-Pauncefote Treaty provides ships safe passage through the Panama Canal.

1904
The Roosevelt Corollary is added to the Monroe Doctrine.

Heroism on the Mound

1902

Heroism on the Mound

After the Spanish-American War, the Philippines became the property of the U.S. Filipino revolutionaries were enraged. They refused to recognize U.S. control and fought hard for independence for three years. The country put its faith in a **provisional** Filipino government in 1898. In February 1899, a Filipino patrol was met with U.S. gunfire. U.S. troops drove the government forces back, and in November, Filipino guerrilla groups took up the fight. Fighting lessened in 1901 with the arrest of rebel leader Emilio Aquinaldo. He pledged allegiance to the U.S., but the conflict continued for another year. The battle ended in 1902, with U.S. forces in control of the archipelago of 7,100 islands. Led by General Arthur MacArthur, the Philippine War was America's first guerrilla conflict in Southeast Asia. The conflict devastated the Philippines. Estimates of casualties range from 50,000 to 2 million. Many people criticized the U.S. for what they saw as a slaughter.

1907

Peace Conference in the Hague

Countries around the world were scrambling to get their hands on more military arms. In 1907, some countries were allotting up to six percent of their national income for the military. This was an incredible ratio in times of peace. On June 15, 1907, representatives of 44 countries came together in The Hague, Netherlands, for a four-month meeting. They wanted to discuss disarming the world.

This was the Second Hague Peace Conference—the first had been held in 1899 and had established international laws and set guidelines for war. The 1907 conference built on what was agreed upon at the first conference. This Second Peace Conference expanded the powers of The Hague court and agreed on the rights and duties of neutral powers in wartime. It also discussed such issues as underwater mines and the practice of converting merchant ships into warships. The building of arms across the globe had prompted this conference, but the issue of disarmament was barely discussed. The representatives recommended that they meet again within seven years. World War I prevented this from happening.

Peace Conference in the Hague

|1906
Roosevelt mediates a dispute between France and Germany at the Algeciras Conference.

|1908
William D'arcy discovers oil in Iran. 45

ACTIVITY
Into the future

Throughout history, the United States has taken an active role in foreign affairs. From the American Revolutionary War to the War in Iraq, the nation has aided in conflict resolution across the globe. In addition to armed conflicts, the United States has been instrumental in encouraging peace agreements between warring nations and provided relief for struggling countries. As one of the most powerful nations in the world, the United States is able to use its influence to guide other countries through difficult times and offer assistance in the form of funds, military action, and mediation.

Every day, United States officials must make decisions about how to react to events taking place around the world. They must carefully look at the details of each event to determine if they should become involved. In some cases, officials disagree about the most suitable course of action. Other times, the case is very clear, and officials quickly put a plan in place.

Once the United States has determined how it will become involved in an international affair, the general public learns the details of the plan. Often, these plans receive wide support from U.S. citizens. However, some actions receive a negative response. These plans become the cause of debates, as people try to determine how the government should respond and why.

Host a Debate

When people have different opinions about a subject, they may host a debate. A debate can be used encourage others to support a specific opinion, subject, or belief. During a debate, individuals or teams present the reasons why they support or oppose a specific subject. Once both sides have presented their case, they can take turns defending any new points that were raised during the initial statements. In the end, the individual or team with the strongest argument is determined to be the winner of the debate.

With a group of friends, try hosting a debate about a foreign affairs subject that is currently in the news. You may choose to debate that the United States should take a different course of action with regard to this subject or that the current plan is appropriate. You may want to propose that the United States offer assistance in a new matter. The opposing team would debate why the United States should remain neutral.

FURTHER
Research

Many books and websites provide information on foreign affairs. To learn more about this topic, borrow books from the library, or surf the Internet.

Books

Most libraries have computers that connect to a database for researching information. If you input a key word, you will be provided with a list of books in the library that contain information on that topic. Non-fiction books are arranged numerically, using their call number. Fiction books are organized alphabetically by the author's last name.

Websites

To learn more about U.S. foreign affairs, visit **www.state.gov**.

For news about events taking place in the United States and around the world, surf to **www.cnn.com**.

Glossary

adversaries: opponents

aggressor: a nation or group that attacks another

communists: people who support a society in which all property is publicly owned and all people are paid according to their skill level and needs

coup: the sudden and forceful overthrowing of a government

exempted: not having to do what others have to do

Federal Reserve: the main banking system of the United States

impeached: charged with misconduct as a public official

imperialistic: countries that acquire and control other countries, often for financial gain

isolationist: someone who believes that one's country should not get involved in the affairs of other countries
isthmus: a narrow strip of land bordered on both sides by water

neutral: a country that does not take part in war

provisional: temporary

quarantined: kept apart; shunned

Shah: king of Iran

sovereignty: independence

successor: a person who comes after another

tariffs: fees or taxes added to imports and exports

terrorist: a person who takes part in extreme acts to promote a political goal

Index